Zoom! Zo

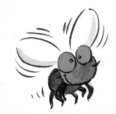

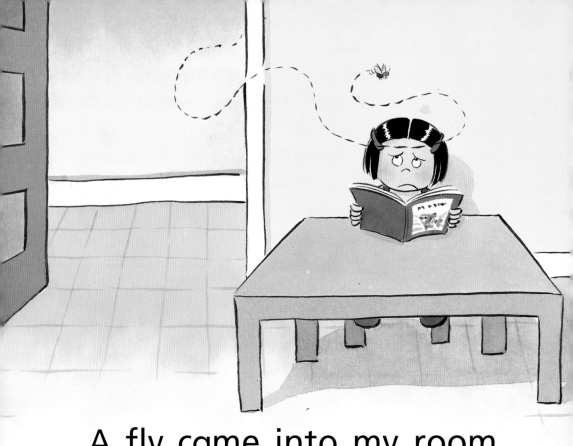

A fly came into my room.

Zoom! Zoom!

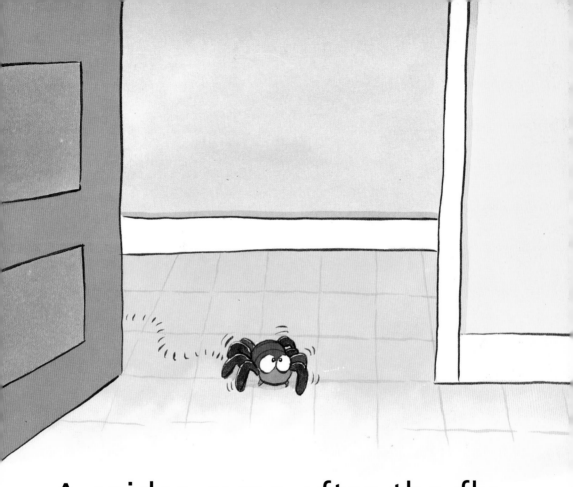

A spider came after the fly.

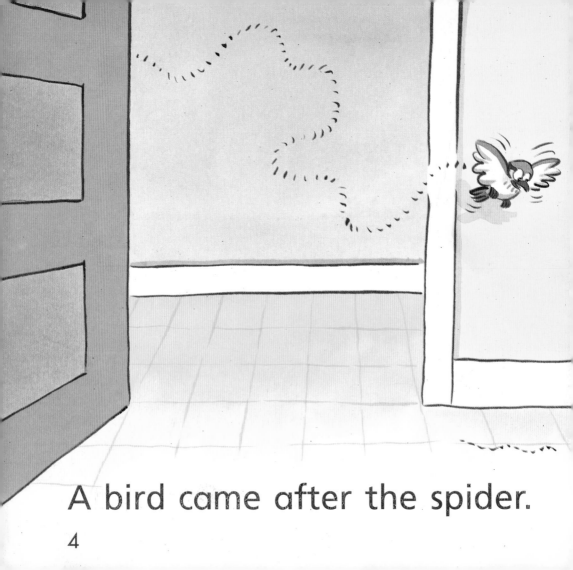

A bird came after the spider.

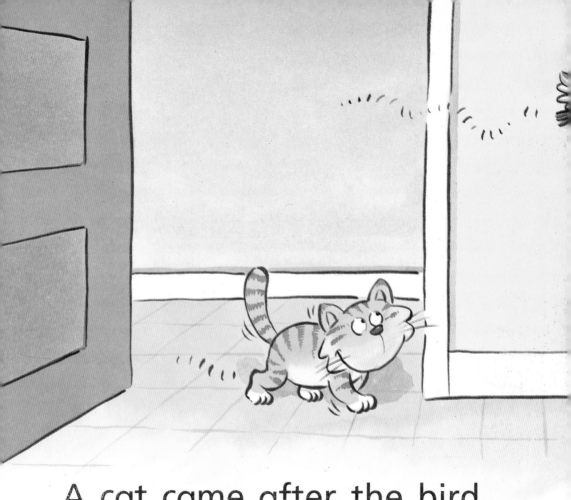

A cat came after the bird.

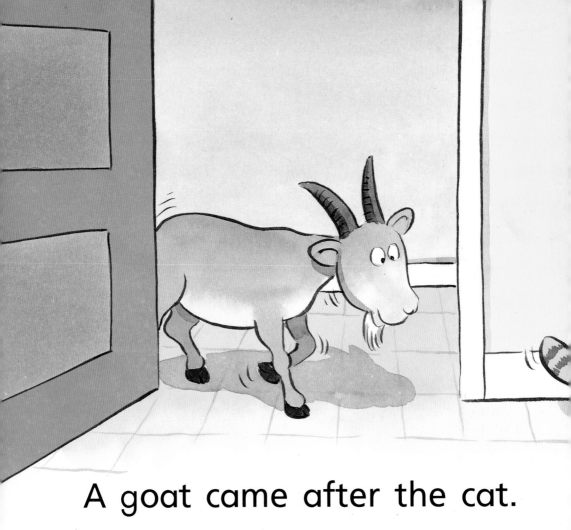

A goat came after the cat.

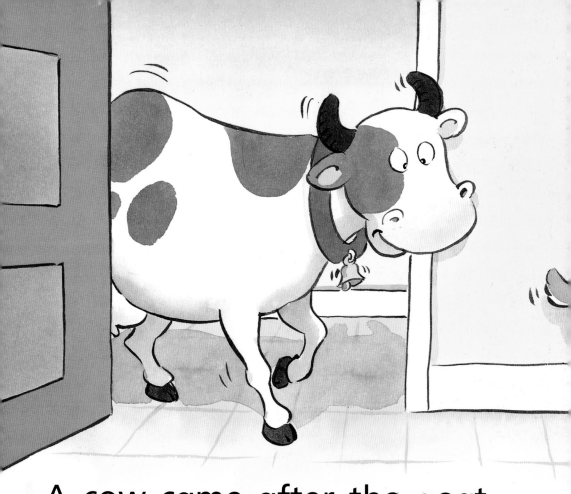

A cow came after the goat.

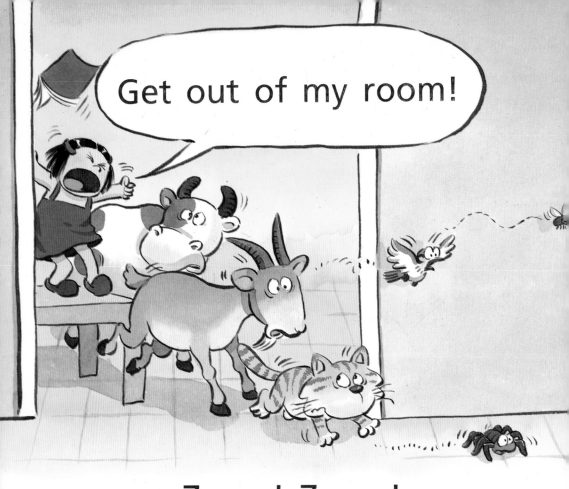

Zoom! Zoom!